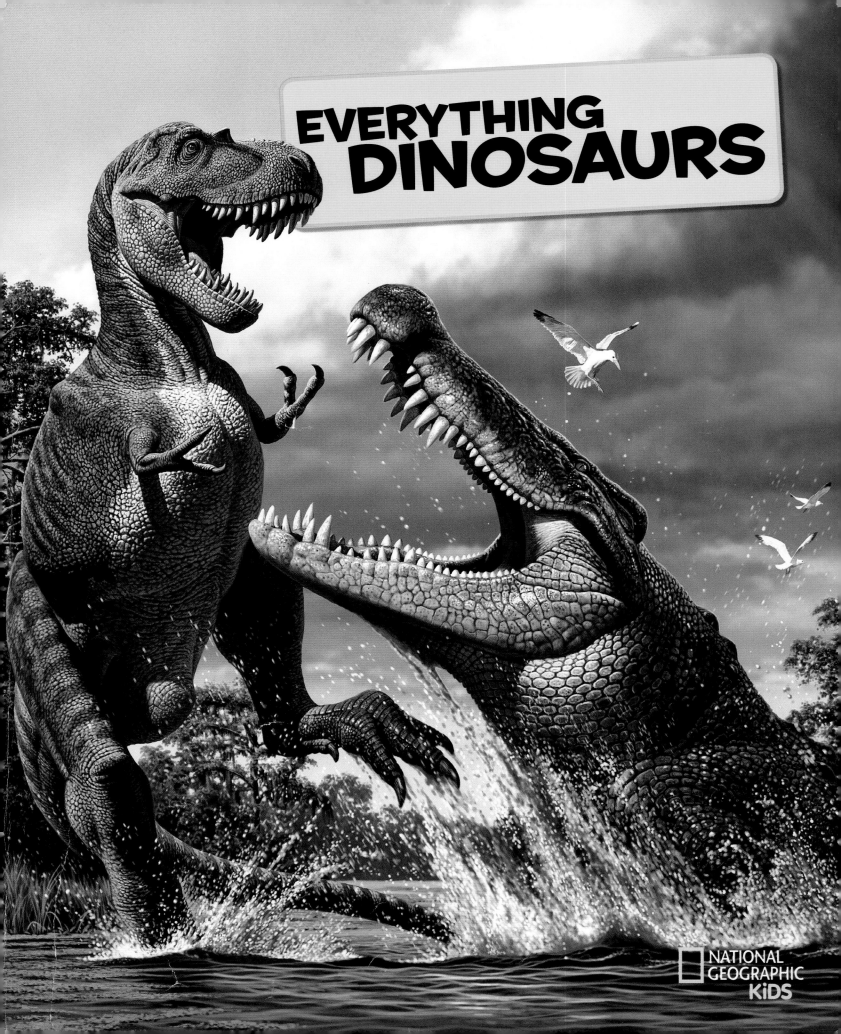

EVERYTHING DINOSAURS

NATIONAL GEOGRAPHIC KiDS

NATIONAL GEOGRAPHIC
WASHINGTON, D.C.

NATIONAL GEOGRAPHIC KiDS

EVERYTHING DINOSAURS

BY BLAKE HOENA

With National Geographic Explorer PAUL SERENO

Illustrations by FRANCO TEMPESTA

CONTENTS

The *Apatosaurus* was a long-necked roamer misnamed the *Brontosaurus*. *Apatosaurus* means "deceptive lizard." It was thought to have migrated in herds.

Bone-headed *Acrotholus audeti* was a small-bodied plant eater that dinosaur scientists believe may have traveled in packs.

INTRODUCTION

WHAT IF DINOSAURS
HADN'T BECOME EXTINCT? CAN YOU

imagine a herd of horned *Triceratops* grazing on the shrubs in your local park? Listen for the distant roar of a hungry *Allosaurus* echoing through the forest. Picture the earth-shaking footfalls of a *Brachiosaurus* as it peeks into a fifth-story window. How would we fit into the world if these gentle giants and ferocious beasts still existed? Maybe that's what fascinates us most about dinosaurs—we don't know. Scientists have dug up fossils and reconstructed how dinosaurs may have looked, but that is only half their story. No one truly knows how they lived or what the world was like with dinosaurs roaming about.

While dinosaurs walked the Earth for 165 million years, much about them is still buried under layers of sedimentary rock. We're still unraveling dinosaur mysteries. Did *Tyrannosaurus rex* hunt in packs like wolves? Were dinosaurs gray-skinned, or did they have colorful scales and feathers? Scientists may not know all there is to know yet, but let's take a look at EVERYTHING we know so far. It's pretty amazing.

EXPLORER'S CORNER

Hi! I'm Dr. Paul Sereno.
I'm a paleontologist, or fossil hunter. For 25 years, I have prowled remote and often barren places on our planet, searching for clues to ancient life. Although dinosaurs are often the target of my expeditions, it turns out that other land animals, such as crocodiles, lived alongside dinosaurs. So, we find these animals, too! As you set off on your journey here into the life and times of dinosaurs, I will pop up in Explorer's Corners here and there to give you tips or clues to a mystery. Off we go!

Diamantinasaurus was a giant sauropod that lived near rivers. It is also the largest dinosaur ever found in Australia.

1

DINOSAURS RULE!

WHAT IS A DINOSAUR?

YOU PROBABLY THINK YOU

ALREADY KNOW, RIGHT? DINOSAURS ARE extinct animals that roamed the Earth millions of years before humans. But that's just the simple answer. What we know about dinosaurs has been pieced together over time.

In the early 1800s, when scientists in England first discovered *Iguanodon* bones, they thought the fossils were simply the remains of a supersized lizard. After all, they named the creature *Iguanodon*, meaning "iguana tooth." Don't make the same mistake! Lizards, snakes, and turtles are not that closely related to dinosaurs, and crocodiles are just distant cousins. Dinosaurs are a very distinct group of animals, even though they had scales and backbones like other reptiles.

Dinosaurs, for the most part, were earthbound. They didn't swim or fly. Dinosaurs stood with their legs directly under them, unlike lizards and crocodiles, which squat down on their legs as they walk. Dinosaurs also walked on their toes, and many paleontologists believe they may have been warm-blooded like their descendants, birds. In many ways, dinosaurs were probably more advanced than some of today's reptiles.

This fast runner was a *Compsognathus,* known to have eaten small prey such as lizards.

DINO BITE MANY SCIENTISTS BELIEVE BIRDS ARE THE LIVING ANCESTORS OF DINOSAURS.

A large meat eater, the *Spinosaurus* used its powerful jaws to snap prey and gulp it down.

HIPS DON'T LIE

Ornithischia, or bird-hipped dinosaurs, such as *Ankylosaurus* and *Triceratops*, were plant eaters. They had hip bones that pointed down and back.

Saurischia, or lizard-hipped dinosaurs, had hip bones that pointed forward. They included all meat eaters and the largest plant eaters.

ORNITHISCHIA

SAURISCHIA

ALL SHAPES AND SIZES

One of the truly amazing things about dinosaurs was how varied they were. From the monstrous *Spinosaurus* to chicken-size predators such as *Compsognathus*, they were a diverse group of animals. It is believed that the variety of dinosaurs rivals that of today's mammals, which range from the largest, the blue whale at 160 tons (145 metric tons), to the smallest, the Etruscan shrew at less than half an ounce (14 g).

WHAT ISN'T A DINOSAUR?

Many people confuse pterosaurs, a group of flying reptiles, and plesiosaurs, a group of marine reptiles, with dinosaurs. These ancient creatures are interesting, but they were not dinosaurs. Dinosaurs could not fly or swim, and are grouped in the ornithischia and saurischia groups. Pterosaurs and plesiosaurs have different ancestors.

DINOSAUR SUPERSTARS

DINOSAURS WERE FIERCE
HUNTERS AND SKILLED FORAGERS, WELL ADAPTED

to the diverse and dangerous world in which they lived. Some were incredibly large, others wore armored plates, and many had voracious appetites. Meet some of the most exceptional dinosaurs, but note that paleontologists make new discoveries every day, which changes what we know about dinosaurs' sizes and habitats.

MOST DANGEROUS

The *Tyrannosaurus rex* was not the largest predator of its day, but it was probably the fiercest. It was smart, with a brain twice the size of most dinosaurs, and a fast hunter. *T. rex* also holds the record for biggest teeth, strongest jaws, and could gulp down 100 pounds (45 kg) of meat in one bite.

BEST DEFENSE

The slow-moving *Ankylosaurus* didn't run from predators—mostly because it couldn't move much faster than a person can walk. But also, few predators could bite through its thick armored plates and pointy spikes. For the persistent predator, *Ankylosaurus* had a club tail to beat off attackers.

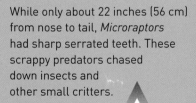

While only about 22 inches (56 cm) from nose to tail, *Microraptors* had sharp serrated teeth. These scrappy predators chased down insects and other small critters.

SMALLEST PREDATOR

DINO BITE   A PALEONTOLOGIST IS A SCIENTIST WHO RESEARCHES PREHISTORIC LIFE.

LARGEST
PREDATOR

LARGEST
PREDATOR

As if one monstrous meat-eating dinosaur wasn't bad enough, the 45-foot-long (14 m), 3-ton (2.7 mt) *Giganotosaurus* probably hunted in packs, which allowed it to take down large prey.

LARGEST
DINOSAUR

Sauropods are a group of giant plant-eating dinosaurs, and the *Argentinosaurus* is possibly the granddaddy of them all. Some may have measured 140 feet (43 m) long and may have weighed in at more than 100 tons (91 mt). It was a true behemoth, but still not the record-holder for largest animal to ever inhabit Earth. That title belongs to the blue whale.

THE AGE OF DINOSAURS

ABOUT 65 MILLION YEARS
AGO, NEARLY 90 PERCENT OF ALL LIVING

things on Earth died. Why? Scientists aren't exactly sure. The mass extinction could have been caused by an asteroid strike or a colossal volcanic eruption. We may never know, but whatever happened marked the end of the age of dinosaurs.

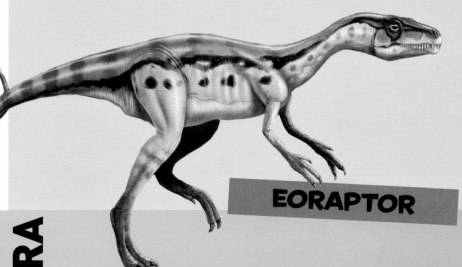

EORAPTOR

THE BEGINNING OF THE END

The massive die-off began in the Mesozoic era, a period of time 251 to 65 million years ago (mya).The Mesozoic era spans the age of dinosaurs. At the time, all of Earth's landmasses were connected in one supercontinent called Pangaea, so dinosaurs dominated from the west coast of what is now North America to the east coast of what is now Asia. They also lumbered about the Arctic as well as what is now Antarctica. The Mesozoic era is divided into three periods. Scientists use rocks and fossils to make these divisions. During each geologic time period, different types of rocks and fossils formed. These depended on the climate and geologic activity, such as volcanic eruptions, and the types of plants and animals that were living in the period.

MESOZOIC ERA

TRIASSIC PERIOD
251–199 MYA

The Triassic period was a time of great change for animal life. The first small mammals scampered about, but this was really a time of reptiles. Flying reptiles took to the sky, and marine reptiles lurked in the oceans. Then, about 230 million years ago, during the Triassic period, the first dinosaurs appeared. They may have been small meat eaters, such as the *Eoraptor*.

JURASSIC PERIOD
199–145 MYA

The Jurassic period was a time of hot, humid weather and rising seas. Huge conifer trees dotted the land. This period gave birth to some of the giants among the dinosaur world. The ground shook as huge plant eaters such as *Brachiosaurus*, *Apatosaurus*, and *Diplodocus* rumbled about pulling leaves from trees. Also during this period, the first birds took flight.

GEO TIME

The Earth is so old that the scientists who study prehistoric life and rocks—paleontologists and geologists—have their own timescale. The geologic timescale measures in leaps of millions of years, or mya for short. Time is divided into eras, periods, and epochs. Dinosaurs were dominant in the Mesozoic era, which has three time periods: Triassic, Jurassic, and Cretaceous.

Life on Earth

Our planet is 4.5 billion years old, but life as we know it has only existed for a brief moment in Earth's history.

CENOZOIC ERA
65 mya–present—Age of Mammals

MESOZOIC ERA
251–65 mya—Age of Reptiles

PALEOZOIC ERA
542–251 mya—Age of Invertebrates, or animals such as reptiles, fish, and amphibians

PRECAMBRIAN
4,500–542 mya—Development of simple organisms to more complex life-forms such as sponges

BRACHIOSAURUS

TYRANNOSAURUS REX

CRETACEOUS PERIOD
145–65 MYA

The Cretaceous period marks the end of the dinosaurs, even though mighty meat eaters such as *Tyrannosaurus rex* and *Spinosaurus* ruled the day. The extinction of dinosaurs brought about the Cenozoic era, also known as the Age of Mammals.

DINO BITE DINOSAURS ROAMED THE EARTH FOR 165 MILLION YEARS. PEOPLE HAVE ONLY BEEN AROUND FOR 100,000.

WHERE IN THE WORLD?

PALEONTOLOGISTS,

THE SCIENTISTS WHO STUDY ancient plants, animals such as dinosaurs, and the climate of the prehistoric past, scour the Earth for fossils and other evidence of ancient life. Some areas of the world shown here are treasure troves of dinosaur fossils.

EXPLORER'S CORNER

When dinosaurs first evolved, they lived on a single supercontinent called Pangaea. As that landmass broke apart, new species evolved on each continent. So, paleontologists have good reason to visit every continent. The best hunting grounds for dinosaur fossils are deserts, such as Mongolia's Gobi or Africa's Sahara. In a desert, there is no soil or greenery to cover the fossils, nearly all of which were buried by rivers long since gone. Ancient lake-bottom deposits, including the famous "feathered dinosaur" beds of northern China, sometimes contain dinosaur skeletons with traces of skin or feathers.

DINOSAUR PROVINCIAL PARK, ALBERTA, CANADA

A treasure chest for paleontologists, up to 40 dinosaur species have been uncovered here, mostly from the late Cretaceous period, such as *Tyrannosaurus rex* and *Ankylosaurus.*

DINOSAUR NATIONAL MONUMENT, UTAH AND COLORADO, U.S.A.

Two complete skulls of a new sauropod, the *Abydosaurus,* from the Cretaceous period were recently discovered here. Other large plant eaters, such as *Diplodocus,* have been dug up here, as well as meat eaters that include *Allosaurus.*

ISCHIGUALASTO PROVINCIAL PARK, SAN JUAN, ARGENTINA

This dry desert area is the location of some of the oldest dinosaur remains of *Herrerasaurus* and *Eoraptors,* from the Triassic period.

C A N A D A
Dinosaur Provincial Park

Dinosaur National Monument

UTAH / COLORADO

UNITED STATES

ARGENTINA
Ischigualasto
Provincial Park

James
Ross
Island

Note: Map shows present-day
country boundaries.

SOLNHOFEN FOSSIL BEDS, BAVARIA, GERMANY

Complete skeletons of **Archaeopteryx** have been unearthed here. This dinosaur may have had the closest relationship to birds of any other theropod.

WEST SUSSEX COUNTY, ENGLAND, U.K.

In 1822, Gideon Mantell discovered giant teeth belonging to an **Iguanodon.** One of the earliest known finds, it led to our modern-day fascination with dinosaurs.

UNITED KINGDOM

GERMANY

Solnhofen Fossil Beds

West Sussex County

C H I N A

Jiufotang Formation

JIUFOTANG FORMATION, LIAONING, CHINA

Many feathered dinosaurs such as the **Microraptor** have been dug up here, leading to theories about how dinosaurs are related to birds.

TANZANIA

Tendaguru Beds

TENDAGURU BEDS, TANZANIA

Rich fossil beds, containing dinosaurs ranging from gigantic plant eaters, like **Brachiosaurus** and **Giraffatitan,** to meat eaters like **Allosaurus** and **Elaphrosaurus,** have been unearthed here.

A U S T R A L I A

Dinosaur Cove

JAMES ROSS ISLAND, ANTARCTICA

The first dinosaur discovered in Antarctica was an ankylosaur, a group of dinosaurs found on every continent except Africa.

A N T A R C T I C A

DINOSAUR COVE, VICTORIA, AUSTRALIA

Dinosaurs from the early Cretaceous period, including small plant eaters like **Leaellynasaura** and **Atlascopcosaurus,** have been discovered at this rich fossil-bearing site.

DINO BITE IN THE 1800s RICHARD OWEN COINED THE TERM "DINOSAUR," WHICH MEANS "TERRIBLE LIZARD."

AN ILLUSTRATED DIAGRAM

DINOSAUR PARTS

MUCH LIKE MAMMALS TODAY, DINOSAURS VARIED IN SIZE, BUILD, AND HABITAT. SOME WERE MEAT EATERS AND some were plant eaters. Some had razor-sharp teeth, while others had no teeth at all. The dinosaurs captured here represent just two of hundreds of different meat eaters and plant eaters of different families and eras: the *Conchoraptor,* a typical meat-eating dromaeosaur and a plant-eating *Stegosaurus*.

STRONG BEAK

The *Conchoraptor* was named for its beak, which was believed to be strong enough to crack open conch and crab shells. The *Conchoraptor* was toothless.

CLAWS

Conchoraptor's claws emerged from flightless and perhaps feathered wings.

CONCHORAPTOR

STEGOSAURUS

HULKING BODY
At 26 to 30 feet (8–9 m), *Stegosaurus*'s enormous size helped protect it from many meat-eating predators.

PLATE BACK
Stegosaurus, the largest plate-backed plant eater, might have used its plates as a cooling mechanism.

SPIKY TAIL
Its spiked tail could have been used as a weapon.

QUADRUPED
Scientists originally thought the *Stegosaurus* walked on two legs. Later research shows it used four legs.

VEGGIE TEETH
Scissor-shaped teeth helped it to eat seeds and leafy plants.

Leaellynasaura was a polar dinosaur that lived in Australia when part of that continent was in the Antarctic Circle. A plant eater, *Leaellynasaura* had large eyes to help it see during the dark months of the year.

2
DINOSAUR LIFE

DINO NURSERY

AT ONE TIME, EXPERTS THOUGHT DINOSAURS, LIKE MANY

modern-day reptiles, did not care for their young. They thought dinosaurs simply laid their eggs in a nest or buried them in the sand, and then stomped off to roar, eat huge meals, and do other dinosaur things. Paleontologists have uncovered evidence that has changed opinions about this old-fashioned idea. When the first fossil of an *Oviraptor* was found in a nest with a clutch of eggs in the Gobi, dinosaur hunters thought it had been killed while stealing eggs from another dinosaur. It was given the name *Oviraptor*, which means "egg thief." But like many early beliefs about dinosaurs, this one proved to be false. The *Oviraptor* most likely died while wrapping its arms around the eggs to protect them.

Today paleontologists believe that most dinosaurs cared for their young. They built nests from plants or dug nests in the ground to lay their eggs in. Smaller dinosaurs brooded their clutch of eggs, much like modern-day birds. However, large sauropods and other giants of the dinosaur world were too massive to sit on their eggs. Rather, they probably covered them with plants or buried them in mud to keep them warm.

Coelophysis fed reptiles to its young.

DINO BITE A YOUNG *TYRANNOSAURUS REX* WAS ABOUT THE SIZE OF A CHICKEN WHEN HATCHED.

EGGS OF ALL SIZES

Dinosaurs laid from a few to two dozen eggs at a time.

THE SKINNY ON EGGS

Meat eaters laid long, thin eggs. Some eggs were about the size of both of your fists put together. Others were bigger.

HAVE A BALL!

Plant eaters laid round eggs. *Diplodocus* eggs were about the size of a bowling ball.

EGG ART

Some dinosaurs organized their eggs into spiral patterns.

After emerging from their nests, young *Mapusaurus* may have traveled and hunted together, learning to survive in groups.

SOME
DINOSAURS
HUNG OUT
IN PACKS.

GROWING UP DINOSAUR

THE AGE OF DINOSAURS WAS A

DANGEROUS TIME TO BE BORN, IF A DINOSAUR EVEN
made it that far. Predators did not wait for eggs to hatch before chowing down, so dinosaurs protected their eggs in hopes that at least a few would hatch. But life didn't get any easier from there. The world was full of dangerous creatures, large and small, looking for a meal. While it is believed that some dinosaurs hatched fully able to walk and fend for themselves, for many, this probably wasn't true.

STICK WITH US

Scientists believe herds of dinosaurs may have migrated seasonally to feeding and breeding grounds. Fossilized footprints of millions of migrating dinosaurs show some traveled with their young. Traveling in a pack would have given younger plant-eating dinosaurs protection from predators.

SHOUT OUTS

The *Parasaurolophus*'s funny head tube may have helped it communicate. There are many theories about the use of the cranial crest, or large tube that curved backward on the *Parasaurolophus*'s head. One is that it made sounds resonate, like blowing in a horn. Another is that it may have helped the *Parasaurolophus* cool down, or it was used to help the dinosaurs, including juvenile or young dinosaurs, recognize each other.

DINO BITE MALE DINOSAURS MAY HAVE ATTRACTED MATES BY BEING MORE COLORFUL THAN THE DRAB FEMALES.

CHOMP OR BE CHOMPED

THEROPODS SUCH AS
HERRERASAURUS AND *CARCHARODONTOSAURUS*
were swift-moving killers who could tackle prey much larger than themselves. Theropods were two-legged, meat-eating dinosaurs who were the most successful hunters.

While most theropods probably didn't hear all that well, their long snouts most likely meant that they relied heavily on a powerful sense of smell to hunt prey.

Theropods such as the *Herrerasaurus* had large, inwardly curving teeth. Once they had a good grip on their prey, there was no getting away.

HERRERASAURUS

They were bipedal, meaning they strode on two feet, which allowed them to run faster than many four-legged plant eaters. While dinosaurs were not speedsters compared to some modern-day animals, a *Compsognathus* could top 30 miles an hour (48 kph). This was fast enough to snatch up small reptiles.

DINO BITE SOME THEROPODS HAD SHORT STUBBY ARMS, WHILE OTHERS HAD SHARP, HOOKED CLAWS.

People once believed that dinosaurs were dumb animals, and while they wouldn't win any spelling bees, it is now believed that theropods, such as the *Troodon*, were intelligent enough to outwit their prey.

CARCHARODONTOSAURUS

Most theropods had long, curved or sharp, serrated teeth. *T. rex* may have had the longest teeth, more than 8 inches (20 cm) long.

With eyes facing forward, similar to modern-day raptors, theropods had binocular vision, meaning both eyes worked together. This allowed them to judge distances and time their attacks.

From the *Carcharodontosaurus* to the monstrous *Giganotosaurus*, many theropods are believed to have hunted in packs. By teaming up, the already sizable *Allosaurus* could possibly take down prey as large as *Diplodocus*.

By the Numbers

1 tooth is all that paleontologists need to identify a dinosaur fossil.

8 inches (20 cm)—the length of a *T. rex* tooth, which was about as long as a large banana

378 teeth in a *Shantungosaurus*'s mouth

THE PLANT EATERS

PLANT-EATING DINOSAURS WERE THE

GENTLE GIANTS OF THE PREHISTORIC ERA, EVEN IF THEY MAY HAVE crushed a fair number of smaller creatures underfoot.

Probably the most familiar plant eaters are the sauropods, which include some of the true giants of the dinosaur world, from the massive *Brachiosaurus* to the even larger *Argentinosaurus*. Why did some of these creatures grow so large? One theory is that they had to. Many of the plants of the Mesozoic era, from fern trees to horsetails, had rough foliage that was difficult to digest. Plant eaters had large digestive tracts to process their food, so they needed larger bodies. Of course, another advantage to being big is that it's a defense against smaller predators.

While meat eaters were built for speed, many plant eaters were slow and lumbering. The thyreophorans, a group of armored dinosaurs, which include the tanklike *Euoplocephalus,* probably ran about as fast as a person walks.

ARGENTINOSAURUS WAS MORE THAN 20 FEET (6 M) HIGH.

STRIP, GRIND, AND SLICE

Sauropods typically had thin, straight teeth. They were designed more for stripping leaves from trees than they were for chewing. Like many modern-day birds, these plant eaters had a stomach part called a gizzard. Their gizzards were filled with stones, which the dinosaurs swallowed. The plant material was ground up as the gizzards churned.

Some of the thyreophorans, such as the *Ankylosaurus,* had small, leaf-shaped teeth for grinding low-growing plants, such as ferns.

The group known as marginocephalians, which includes the *Triceratops,* had rows of tiny teeth in the back of their mouths, sometimes numbering in the hundreds. Their chisel-like teeth were perfect for slicing through plant leaves and stalks.

VEGETARIAN VS. CARNIVORE

A *Brachiosaurus* skull shows the teeth of a plant-eating sauropod. This tall giant had spoon-shaped teeth suited to eating tree leaves.

Sharp-edged *T. rex* chompers were built for tearing and eating meat. Each one was banana-size.

Giraffes would be envious of the *Mamenchisaurus*, which had a neck that could stretch 35 feet (11 m) long.

WHAT'S FOR LUNCH?

It's hard to know for sure what any dinosaur ate unless you have the remains of a fossilized stomach or coprolites (fossilized dung) that show digested food. Paleontologists use these, as well as the type of teeth and information about the dinosaur's habitat, to piece together its regular dining habits. Different plants grew in different eras. Flowering plants, for example, did not evolve until the Cretaceous period. Here are some likely foods of the dinosaur vegetarians:

- FERNS
- MONKEY PUZZLE TREES (EVERGREENS)
- CYCADS (WOODY STEMMED PLANTS AND TREES)
- HORSETAILS (WEED-LIKE PLANTS)
- CONIFERS
- GINKGOES (TREES)

DINO BITES DUCK-BILLED *IGUANODONS* HAD JAWS THAT MOVED UP AND DOWN AND SIDE TO SIDE AS THEY ATE.

AN ILLUSTRATED GALLERY

AWESOME CREATURES

SPECTACULAR AND DIVERSE, DINOSAURS are interesting and attractive because we can only imagine how they lived. Our knowledge comes from piecing together scientific evidence from their fossils and their habitats on prehistoric Earth.

The thick skull of the *Pachycephalosaurus* may have been a sign of maturity or it may have been handy in battle.

Nothronychus was a plant eater discovered in 2011.

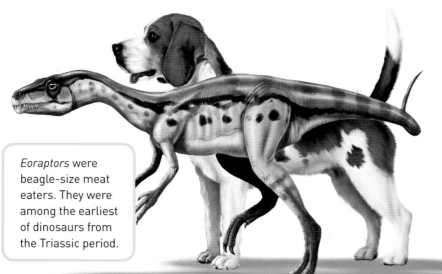

Eoraptors were beagle-size meat eaters. They were among the earliest of dinosaurs from the Triassic period.

Paleontologists rarely discover complete dinosaur skeletons. Instead, dinosaurs are constructed from scattered parts. Museums such as the Carnegie Museum of Natural History in Pittsburgh, Pennsylvania, use fossils and fossil replicas for display. Fossil replicas are plastic reproductions that are lighter and sturdier than the real thing.

Muttaburrasaurus was a dinosaur named after the small Australian town, Muttaburra, where its fossil remains were found in 1963.

Four-legged Rebbachisaurus had a long neck and tail.

Despite fossils showing they had feathers and wings, *Ornithomimus* could not fly. They were speedy runners with keen sight.

3

DIGGING UP DINOS

ALL IN THE FAMILY

THE DINOSAUR FAMILY TREE IS A COMPLICATED
ONE. THERE WAS PROBABLY AS WIDE A VARIETY OF DINOSAURS IN THE MESOZOIC
era as there are mammals today. The dinosaur era also spanned 165 million years!

ORNITHISCHIA
Ornithischia, or bird-hipped dinosaurs, lived from the early Jurassic period to the end of the Cretaceous period.

DINOSAURIA

THYREOPHORANS
Thyreophorans were a group of armored dinosaurs that lived from the early Jurassic to the end of the Cretaceous period.

- *Stegosaurus* (Late Jurassic)
- *Minmi* (Early Cretaceous)
- *Euoplocephalus* (Late Cretaceous)
- *Ankylosaurus* (Late Cretaceous)

CERAPODA
Cerapoda is the ancestor group of ornithopods and marginocephalians. Ornithopods were the largest and longest lived of the ornithischia. They were a group of plant eaters that walked on two legs and lived from the late Jurassic to the end of the Cretaceous period.

- *Ouranosaurus* (Early Cretaceous)
- *Iguanodon* (Early Cretaceous)
- *Maiasaura* (Late Cretaceous)

MARGINOCEPHALIANS
Marginocephalians were plant eaters with bony structures on their skulls. They lived from the late Jurassic to the end of the Cretaceous period.

- *Triceratops* (Late Cretaceous)
- *Microceratus* (Late Cretaceous)

OURANOSAURUS

TRICERATOPS

SAURISCHIA

Saurischia, or the lizard-hipped dinosaurs, lived from the late Triassic period to the end of the Cretaceous period.

ARGENTINOSAURUS

THEROPODS

Theropods were the main predators of the day. They were also intelligent dinosaurs and spanned the entire Age of Dinosaurs.

- *Herrerasaurus* (Late Triassic)
- *Eoraptor* (Late Triassic)
- *Coelophysis* (Late Triassic)

SAUROPODS

Sauropods were large, long-necked plant eaters, living from the early Jurassic to the end of the Cretaceous period.

- *Apatosaurus* (Late Jurassic)
- *Brachiosaurus* (Late Jurassic)
- *Diplodocus* (Late Jurassic)
- *Argentinosaurus* (Late Cretaceous)

ORNITHOMIMUS

- *Compsognathus* (Late Jurassic)
- *Ornithomimus* (Late Cretaceous)
- *Sinornithomimus* (Late Cretaceous)

TETANURANS

Tetanurans were stiff-tailed dinosaurs that first appeared in the Jurassic period.

- *Megalosaurus* (Late Jurassic)
- *Allosaurus* (Late Jurassic)
- *Spinosaurus* (Late Cretaceous)

TYRANNOSAURS

- *Dilong* (Early Cretaceous)
- *Tyrannosaurus rex* (Late Cretaceous)

DEINONYCHOSAURS

- *Archaeopteryx* and all other birds (Late Jurassic)
- *Deinonychus* (Early Cretaceous)
- *Microraptor* (Early Cretaceous)
- *Oviraptor* (Late Cretaceous)
- *Troodon* (Late Cretaceous)
- *Velociraptor* (Late Cretaceous)

OVIRAPTOR

MEGALOSAURUS

FOSSIL HUNTING

DON'T THINK IT IS ONLY PALEONTOLOGISTS WHO MAKE IMPORTANT

fossil finds. Sometimes people stumble upon dinosaur fossils on their properties. Amateur fossil hunters have discovered bone fragments and preserved tracks. One dinosaur hunter found the fossil of a new species of ankylosaur while on a walk near his home in Maryland, U.S.A. Whether an amateur or a professional, dinosaur hunters need a keen eye and knowledge of the rocks in their "hunting" area.

DINOS IN YOUR BACKYARD?

Dinosaur parks are sometimes located in lands where dinosaurs once roamed. Some parks, such as the Stonerose fossil site in Washington State, U.S.A., or Dinosaur Provincial Park in Alberta, Canada, have guided tours where you can join digs. Visitors to Naracoorte Caves National Park in South Australia can tour caves where fossils have been found. There are also major fossil sites on every continent. But you don't need to venture far. Some sites are in our backyards. If you live in an area with the right environment and where the rocks formed in the dinosaur age, you might have a buried fossil treasure within reach.

TOOLS OF THE TRADE

In the "field," or out digging things up, paleontologists use a number of tools to unearth their discoveries, such as picks and shovels. In the lab, they use tools such as cameras and scanners to take images of the outside and inside of a fossil.

PICKS are for digging and splitting rock.

DRILLS AND JACKS are tools that use air pressure to remove hard material surrounding bones.

CHISELS AND HAMMERS are used to split rocks and chip away at delicate material.

MAGNIFIERS are for looking closely at fossils and specimens.

SAFETY GOGGLES protect eyes from debris that flies up when hammering or drilling.

BRUSHES whisk dust and debris away.

DINO BITE IT CAN TAKE MONTHS TO YEARS TO REMOVE FOSSILIZED BONES FROM THE ROCK THAT THEY'RE EMBEDDED IN.

Fossils are the preserved remains of prehistoric plants and animals. When paleontologists find a fossil, they mark the site out in a grid so the bones can be taken in order.

TYPES OF FOSSILIZATION

PERMINERALIZATION occurs after a dinosaur is buried, when water pushes minerals into the porous spaces of its body parts. Even bones are not completely solid, so water seeps into them, too. The minerals then harden, leaving behind everything from complete skeletons to pieces of teeth or traces of feathers.

REPLACEMENT, or petrification, happens when plant material is slowly, molecule by molecule, replaced by minerals. Petrified wood is an example of this process.

CASTS AND MOLDS occur after a shell is buried in sediment. It dissolves and leaves behind an impression of itself in rock. This "mold" then fills in with minerals that harden into a copy, or "cast," of the shell.

When a dinosaur died of natural causes (as in it didn't get chomped and chewed by a meat eater), its head and tail curled back, almost forming a circle with its body. Paleontologists know this from finding complete fossilized dinosaur skeletons like this *Archaeopteryx.*

CLAWS, TAILS, AND SAILS

OVER MILLIONS
OF YEARS, DINOSAURS HAVE
adapted to the world around them. Sauropods developed long necks to reach leaves high up in trees. Theropods grew razor-sharp claws and teeth to catch prey. Thyreophorans sported armor to protect themselves against those very sharp claws and teeth. But it's not always clear what some of the stranger adaptations were used for.

EXPLORER'S CORNER

Flesh, horns, feathers, scales—these are much softer than bone and rarely preserved as more than an outline, if at all, in fossils. Paleontologists reconstruct them using living reptiles and birds as a guide. Loose flesh covers smooth bone, whereas horns, feathers, and large scales often cover bone that has a telling texture. Dinosaur body color remains largely guesswork.

CRAZY CLAWS

Deinonychus earned their name "terrible claws" because of long sickle-shaped claws on their hind feet. While hunting, *Deinonychus* most likely grasped their prey with their clawed hands while slashing with their hind claws.

DINO BITE *Triceratops* had a beaked mouth, with jaws strong enough to crush bone.

POINTY HORNS

Triceratops horns might not have been used for defense. After all, if one poked and killed a *Tyrannosaurus rex*, the taller *T. rex* would fall over onto the *Triceratops*. Not good! The horns could have been a sign of maturity. Forward curving horns showed that a *Triceratops* was an adult and ready to mate.

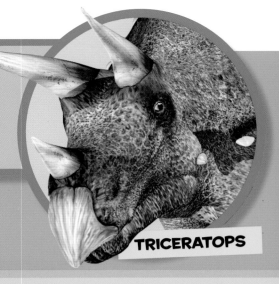

TRICERATOPS

WINGED WARRIORS

Some dinosaurs such as the *Microraptor* had feathered wings. They also had long grasping claws. While they couldn't fly, they most likely were able to climb tall trees and glide like a flying squirrel. This might be how they hunted.

TERRIFIC TAILS

All dinosaurs had tails. Theropods may have used theirs to balance while running, but some other dinosaurs had more unique uses for theirs.

WHIP IT! At more than 40 feet (12 m) long, the *Diplodocus*'s tail may have been longer than any other dinosaur's. Not only did it have a long tail, but the tail was strong and heavy. *Diplodocus* may have used its tail like a whip to snap at predators and scare them off.

SPIKE IT! A *Stegosaurus*'s spiked tail was deadly. The end of the tail had four spikes sticking out of the sides, and the *Stegosaurus* would swing it around at attacking predators.

DIPLODOCUS

STEGOSAURUS

FEATHERED FRIENDS?

One function of feathers is to help birds to fly, but dinosaurs may have had feathers for another purpose. The flight feathers of birds are evenly long and stiff to help give birds lift. Instead, most dinosaur feathers were downy and less even. These feathers probably trapped air next to their bodies to help keep them warm.

PRETTY SAILS

Spinosaurus was one of the biggest predators. It also had one of the oddest body parts: a sail on its back that stood as tall as 6 feet (1.8 m). We don't know for sure, but the sail may have scared off enemies by making the *Spinosaurus* look bigger. The brightly colored sail may have been used to attract a mate, or it may have absorbed sunlight and helped the *Spinosaurus* stay warm.

EXPLORER'S CORNER

No species can plan in advance for something as rare as a giant asteroid. The dusty, dark, and cold period of time that followed the great impact 65 million years ago changed the world. It wiped out every land animal larger than an average-size dog, including the last and some of the greatest dinosaurs such as *Triceratops* and *T. rex*.

DINO BITE SCIENTISTS CALL THE DEATH OF THE DINOSAURS A MASS EXTINCTION, SINCE SO MANY TYPES OF ANIMALS DIED.

END OF THE DINOSAURS

THE END OF THE DINOSAURS IS A MYSTERY BECAUSE WE STILL DON'T KNOW EXACTLY WHY THEY

became extinct. What we do know is that something disastrous happened. Paleontologists aren't sure exactly what, but there are two basic theories, or ideas, about how they became extinct. One idea is that an outside force caused the death of the dinosaurs, and another is that a catastrophic earthly event occurred.

SUDDEN IMPACT

A huge asteroid may have hit Earth 65 million years ago. The impact is believed to have destroyed everything within hundreds of miles, and kicked up enough dust and debris to block out the sun and cause the planet to cool. A crater more than 100 miles (161 km) wide in the Yucatán Peninsula in Mexico may be the impact site. The chances of it happening again are very small.

A PLANET IN TURMOIL

Another possibility is that huge volcanoes spewed enough ash and soot to block out the sun, making the world too cold for dinosaurs, and the food they ate, to survive. Scientists are fairly certain that the Cretaceous period was a time of high volcanic activity.

Dinosaurs weren't the only ones to die. It is estimated that about three quarters of all living things perished at this time, from large marine reptiles, such as the *Plesiosaurus*, to insects, fish, and plants. While smaller reptiles, birds, amphibians, and mammals were also affected by this event, many adapted to the new conditions. Mammals seemed to fare the best, as they soon flourished.

SHOCK WAVES

On February 15, 2013, a meteor streaked across the skies of Russia, exploding 15 miles (24 km) above the city of Chelyabinsk. Shock waves blew out windows, injuring 1,500 people. This was a small meteor compared to the one that may have killed the dinosaurs.

DINOSAUR COMPARISONS

HUMANS VS. DINOS

DINOSAURS COME IN ALL SIZES, from giant sauropods to small raptors. How would you stack up against some of them?

By the Numbers

3 miles an hour (4.8 kph) —how fast *Ankylosaurus* could run

10 miles an hour (16 kph) —how fast a stampeding *Diplodocus* could run

20 miles an hour (30 kph) —how fast *T. rex* could run

24 miles an hour (39 kph) —how fast a *Velociraptor* could run

The *Triceratops* had a skull about 8 feet (2.5 m) long, accounting for about a third of its length. That would be like you having a head two and a half times its current size.

VELOCIRAPTOR

Reaching speeds of 24 miles an hour (39 kph), a running *Velociraptor* could keep up with a slow-moving car.

TYRANNOSAURUS REX

T. rex could gulp down about 100 pounds (45 kg) of meat in one mouthful. That would be equal to you stuffing 300 hamburgers into your mouth at one time.

DIPLODOCUS

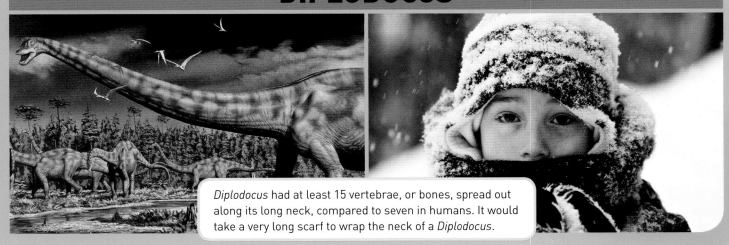

Diplodocus had at least 15 vertebrae, or bones, spread out along its long neck, compared to seven in humans. It would take a very long scarf to wrap the neck of a *Diplodocus*.

With its unicorn-like crest, the *Tsintaosaurus* would have been quite beautiful to behold. A plant eater, the *Tsintaosaurus* lived in herds and walked on all fours.

FUN WITH DINOS

WHAT KIND OF DINO ARE YOU?

DINOSAUR FANS AREN'T SHY ABOUT
PICKING THEIR FAVORITE PREHISTORIC CREATURES. BUT HAVE YOU
ever thought about what kind of dinosaur you are most like? Take this quiz and find out.

1 You have a reputation as a:

A. Bossy pants with a nasty bite
B. Person of action
C. A bit of a hardhead

2 Which lifestyle do you prefer?

A. A slow stroll
B. Life in the fast lane
C. Hanging with my peeps

3 When your belly growls, you prefer to:

A. Gnaw on a rare steak
B. Sink your teeth into a juicy burger with lettuce, tomato, and a side of fries
C. Chomp on a giant salad

4 For fun, you like to:

A. Scavenge through the refrigerator
B. Travel in packs with friends
C. Collect hats

5 Would you rather be noticed for:

A. Your healthy smile
B. The feathers you like to wear
C. Your famous name

EXPLORER'S CORNER

The sail-backed *Spinosaurus* tops my list of weird dinosaurs. While its skull shape resembled a crocodile's, the 6-foot-tall (1.8 m) sail on its back would hardly allow it to hide in shallow water. The long raking hand claws and short hind legs suggest a special lifestyle close to the water's edge, stalking and perhaps swimming after large fish.

YOU AS A DINO

Yeah, sure you're an individual, just like the hundreds of different kinds of dinosaurs. But what kind of dinosaur is most like you? See for yourself:

IF YOU SCORED MOSTLY
A You're a sharp-toothed, meat-eating tyrant lizard—a *T. rex*.

IF YOU SCORED MOSTLY
B You're a fast and omnivorous *Struthiomimus*.

IF YOU SCORED MOSTLY
C Don't let it go to your pretty head, but you're a plant-eating *Dracorex* (named after a *Harry Potter* character).

EVEN MIX You're an unusual and yet undiscovered hybrid dinosaur!

STRUTHIOMIMUS

DRACOREX

TYRANNOSAURUS REX

DINO BITE SCIENTISTS AREN'T SURE, BUT *DRACOREX* MIGHT BE A JUVENILE *PACHYCEPHALOSAURUS.*

DINOSAURS IN CULTURE

OUR GREAT
FASCINATION WITH dinosaurs has sparked several blockbuster movies, but adventure movies often confuse science fiction with science fact.

DON'T MIX THE DNA

The three *Jurassic Park* films are probably the most famous dinosaur movies. In the movies, dinosaur DNA has been extracted from a mosquito trapped in amber, or fossilized tree resin, from the Jurassic period. A very creative idea, but keep in mind that DNA deteriorates over time. It is highly unlikely that any could survive completely intact for millions and millions of years, no matter how well it was preserved. Plus, when scientists collect the dinosaur DNA, they could accidently extract some mosquito DNA, mixing the two, and then scientists would have created a true monster, a *Mosquitosaurus rex!*

Humans are threatened by a *T. Rex* in a scene from the first *Jurassic Park* movie.

HAVE WE MET BEFORE?

There have now been four movies in the *Ice Age* series, which tells of the adventures of a hapless sloth named Sid and his friends Manny the woolly mammoth and Diego the saber-toothed cat. And even though they would never have encountered dinosaurs (mammoths and saber-toothed cats would have lived millions of years ago, while dinosaurs lived tens of millions of years ago), in *Dawn of the Dinosaurs*, the friends find a world of lost dinosaurs.

YOU'RE FROM WHERE?

In *King Kong* (2005), a mysterious island is discovered where prehistoric creatures live. One of them is King Kong, a giant ape, but there are also dinosaurs that escaped extinction. Early in the movie, King Kong battles a *Vastatosaurus rex*, a fictional descendent of *T. rex*. While there may be parts of the ocean that are yet unexplored, the idea that a large island could go unnoticed with modern-day mapping and satellites is pretty far-fetched.

DINO BITE   THE REX IN *T. REX* MEANS "KING."

IT'S ALL SCIENCE FICTION

If *Jurassic Park* remained true to its name and included dinosaurs from only the Jurassic period, which of these creatures should not have appeared in the movie?

  Tyrannosaurus rex—While one of the best known dinosaurs, it was actually from the Cretaceous period.

 **Dilophosaurus**—These predators were from the Jurassic period, but there is no proof that they sprayed venom like in the movie.

 **Velociraptor**—Even though these predators appear in all three *Jurassic Park* movies, they are from the late Cretaceous period.

Triceratops—These are also from the late Cretaceous, but they are probably the best known dinosaur after *T. rex.*

 **Stegosaurus**—This Jurassic dinosaur had a spiked tail and bony plates along its back.

  **Brachiosaurus**—One of the true giants of the Jurassic period, this dinosaur stretched 85 feet (26 m) long and stood 50 feet (15 m) tall.

 **Parasaurolophus**—This duck-billed dinosaur from the late Cretaceous period earned a spot in the movie as a *T. rex* snack.

  **Compsognathus**—This small meat eater from the Jurassic period was given the nickname "Chompy" in the movie.

DINOSAUR ROAD TRIP

DINOSAURS "LIVE" IN THE WORLD ONLY IN OUR IMAGINATIONS.

Their fossilized remains are dug up throughout the world. Their skeletons are displayed in museums, and their models are hits at dinosaur parks. Pack your bags for this time-traveling road trip!

Dinosaur National Monument has fossil beds that were first excavated in 1909.

Welcome to
DINOSAUR, COLORADO
Gateway to
DINOSAUR NATIONAL MONUMENT

Dinosaur parks are theme parks where life-size sculptures of dinosaurs are displayed. Visitors to the Finnish Science Centre in Vantaa, Finland, are given a guided tour of the sculptures.

DINO BITES ONLY ABOUT 2,000 NEARLY COMPLETE DINOSAUR SKELETONS EXIST IN THE WORLD.

This sand-sculpture dinosaur was created for beachgoers in Fulong, Taiwan.

FOSSIL ID

MATCH EACH FOSSIL TO THE DINOSAUR IT COMES FROM.

Answers at the bottom of the page.

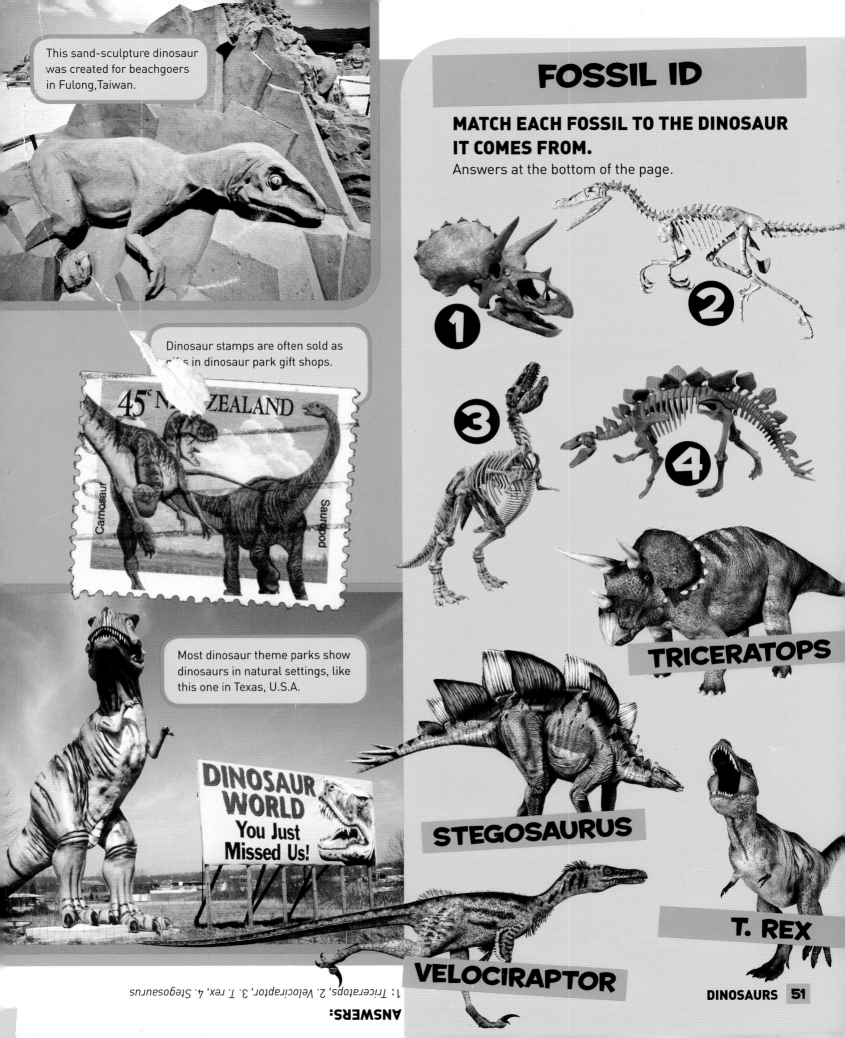

1

2

3

4

Dinosaur stamps are often sold as gifts in dinosaur park gift shops.

45ᶜ NEW ZEALAND

Carnosaur

Sauropod

Most dinosaur theme parks show dinosaurs in natural settings, like this one in Texas, U.S.A.

DINOSAUR WORLD
You Just Missed Us!

TRICERATOPS

STEGOSAURUS

T. REX

VELOCIRAPTOR

ANSWERS: 1: Triceratops, 2. Velociraptor, 3. T. rex, 4. Stegosaurus

DINOSAUR OR NOT?

PALEONTOLOGISTS ARE
CONSTANTLY UNEARTHING NEW TRUTHS ABOUT
dinosaurs. New research has helped eliminate some old ideas as false. Can you guess which of these are false and which are true?

(A) PTERODACTYL — Early in the Mesozoic era, this dinosaur ruled the sky.

(B) BRONTOSAURUS — This is one of the most famous dinosaur species.

(C) UTAHRAPTOR — Unlike other reptiles, this feathered hunter dinosaur was most likely warm-blooded.

(D) PLESIOSAUR — This huge ocean dinosaur lived from the Jurassic to the Cretaceous period.

A. FALSE—Pterosaurs are a group of flying reptiles. Pterodactyls are just one of many pterosaurs. They are not dinosaurs. They also most likely did not have feathers, and they are not related to birds.

B. FALSE—Othniel Charles Marsh was one of the top paleontologists of his day, but he made a colossal mistake when it came to the *Brontosaurus*. He discovered and named *Apatosaurus*, a large plant-eating dinosaur, in the late 1800s. A few years later he received bones of a larger plant-eating dinosaur, which he thought was a different species. He named it *Brontosaurus*. Nearly 100 years later, paleontologists realized the first *Apatosaurus* bones were probably from a juvenile dinosaur, while the later bones were from an adult.

DINO BITE WE DON'T KNOW FOR SURE WHAT DINOSAUR SKIN LOOKED LIKE, AS SKIN DOES NOT FOSSILIZE.

C. TRUE—They laid eggs and ran on two back legs like other theropods. *Utahraptor* almost could be mistaken for a bird if not for its height of 20 feet (6 m).

D. FALSE—Dinosaurs lived on land. Plesiosaurs were marine reptiles that grew to more than 40 feet (12 m) long.

STARS OF PALEONTOLOGY

JACK HORNER

JACK HORNER is a rock star among paleontologists. In 1975, he discovered a large *Maiasaura* nesting site, which proved that some dinosaurs cared for their young.

ROBERT BAKKER is the author of the book *The Dinosaur Heresies* (1986), in which he proposed the idea that dinosaurs were warm-blooded. One argument behind his theory is that birds are warm-blooded and descendants of dinosaurs, so most likely dinosaurs were warm-blooded as well.

XU XING uncovered many feathered dinosaurs throughout the 1990s and early 2000s. These discoveries helped promote the idea that birds descended from dinosaurs.

YOUR DINOSAUR NAME

When a paleontologist finds a fossil of a yet undiscovered animal, they often get to name it. Sometimes they use ancient Greek words, like in "tyrannosaur," which would break down into *tyrannos* for "tyrant" and *saurus* for "lizard," to describe a feature of the dinosaur. Other times they use someone else's name. If you found a dinosaur, what would it be called? Follow these steps to find out:

1 Take the last name of someone you admire (or who is famous).

2 Then add words describing something about that person, such as why they are famous.

3A If you think they are a carnivore, add "raptor" to the end.

3B If you think they eat both vegetables and meat, add "osaurus" to the end.

3C If they eat only plants, add "ocus" to the end.

For example, the author of this book would name a dinosaur he discovered after his favorite author, J. R. R. Tolkien, who wrote *The Hobbit*:

TOLKIENWRITEROSAURUS

HOW DINOSAURS FIRST
EVOLVED AND HOW THEY BECAME EXTINCT

millions of years later remain two of their greatest mysteries. We know they first evolved about 230 million years ago looking pretty much like *Eoraptor*, a 3-foot-long (0.9 m), two-legged dinosaur I discovered in Argentina. Millions of years would pass, however, before dinosaurs ruled the land as the largest plant and meat eaters.

We also know that the collision of the Earth with a giant asteroid was the main cause for the disappearance of dinosaurs 65 million years ago. Now we know that some descendants of the dinosaurs survived. We call them birds. Birds share many things with *T. rex* and relatives from the dinosaur era, including feathers and nests where they lay hard-shelled eggs.

I am most interested in other unanswered questions about dinosaurs, such as how some of them grew larger than elephants, why none of them lived in trees like a gorilla, or in the water like a whale, and how they were able to cross oceans from one continent to another. I am also interested in how they ate tough plants, how agile they were, and how they took to the air as birds. I wonder how smart they were compared to a mammal.

Dinosaur fossils that await discovery around the world will help solve these mysteries—along with you, the next generation of paleontologists who will discover them!

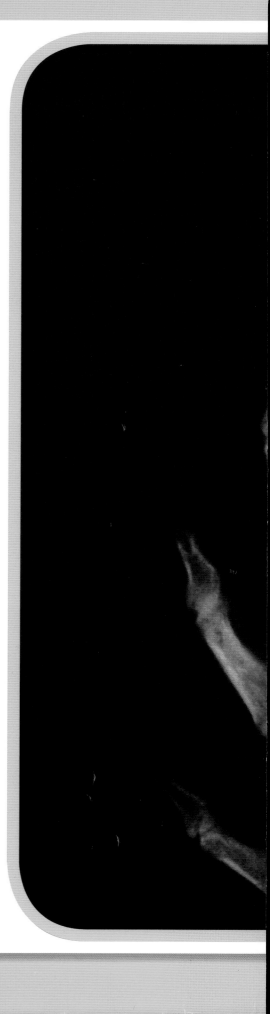

Using CT scans, scientists can look inside the skull of the dawn dinosaur, *Eoraptor*, as well as the hand of the paleontologist who discovered it!

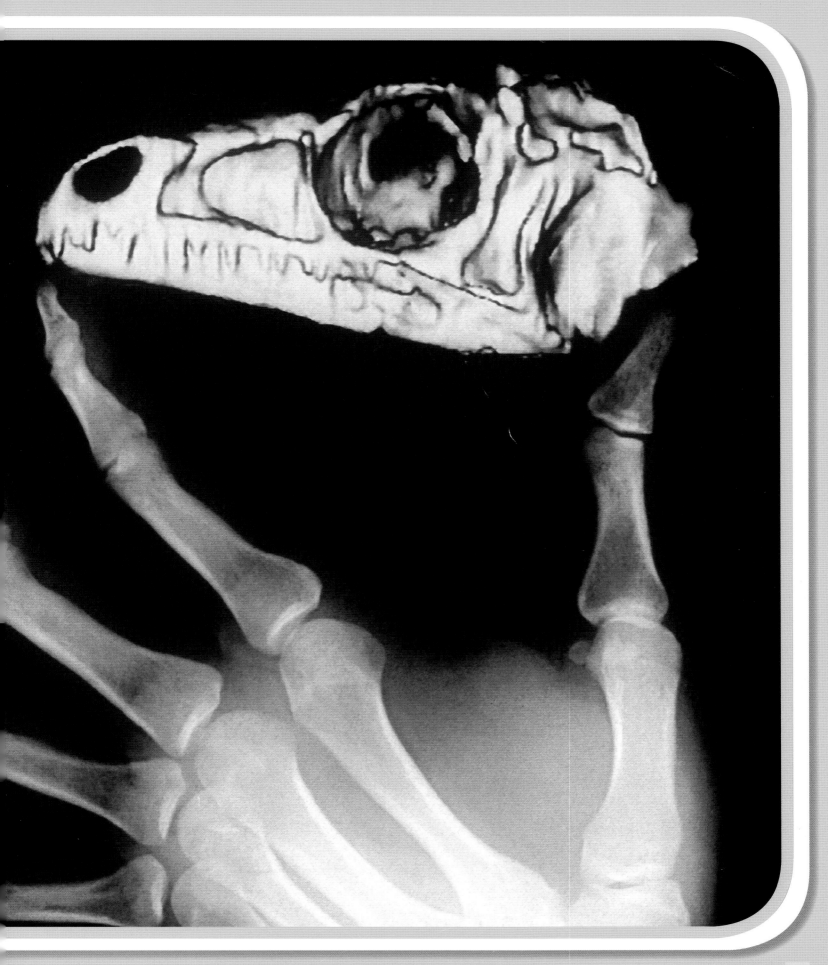

AFTERWORD

THEY WERE CARNIVOROUS

BEASTS—FIERCE AND VORACIOUS. THEY WERE ALSO herbivores and lumbering giants—gentle and striking. They inspire our imaginations and our fears. But not only that, they may provide clues into how humans, as well as other animals, evolved. Learning why dinosaurs grew horns or how they developed feathers may help scientists better understand why some animals living today have certain traits. Studying dinosaurs may also help us understand how to survive in a world with changing climate conditions.

We hear about climate change in the news almost daily. While scientists don't all agree on the cause, most believe that our big blue home is getting warmer. Ice caps are melting, and wildlife habitats are changing. Paleontologists look at changes in climate over time spans of many millions of years. Understanding how these forces, such as loss of habitat and food sources, drove some animals to extinction may help us understand how to survive in a warmer world.

With thousands of fossils unearthed every year, who knows what exciting things scientists will learn about the past and what amazing new theories they may present. Our futures could depend on their research.

ON DISPLAY

Don't touch! Dinosaur fossils are fragile. After all, they are millions and millions of years old. Paleontologists take great care in removing them from the ground, and they may spend months cleaning the bones with small picks, brushes, and acid. They then identify the bones and figure out how they are pieced together.

Many of their finds are simply pieces of vertebrae or teeth or chunks of skulls. Most of the dinosaur bones that have been found are stored in museums, and only paleontologists have access to them.

Since unearthed dinosaur bones are so fragile, what you see in a museum may actually not be real bones, especially if it's a full skeleton. Instead, museum curators make molds and casts of fossils to create their displays so visitors can see what dinosaurs were like.

This hefty fellow is a *Tarchia*, a plant-eating ankylosaur that weighed up to 10,000 pounds (4,536 kg).

A *Deinonychus* rips into its dinner with its razor teeth. This Cretaceous period dinosaur had a talon claw on its hind feet.

AN INTERACTIVE GLOSSARY

DINO TALK

Known as the "earthquake lizard," the *Seismosaurus* is one of the longest dinosaurs, measuring up to 110 feet (34 m) in length.

THESE WORDS ARE COMMONLY
USED WHEN PEOPLE TALK ABOUT AND STUDY DINOSAURS.

Use the glossary to learn what each word means and visit the page numbers listed to see the word used in context. Then test your dinosaur knowledge!

1. Bipedal
An animal that walks on two legs
(PAGE 26)

Which dinosaurs were bipedal?
a. *Iguanodon*
b. *Ankylosaurus*
c. *Spinosaurus*
d. *Diplodocus*

2. Carnivore
An animal with a diet consisting mostly of other animals
(PAGES 28, 53)

Which dinosaurs were carnivores?
a. *Mapusaurus*
b. *Argentinosaurus*
c. *Giganotosaurus*
d. *Dracorex*

3. Era
A period of time in Earth's geological history when certain features, such as a type of rock or certain animals and plants, were dominant
(PAGES 14–15)

Dinosaurs lived during which era?
a. Cenozoic
b. Paleozoic
c. Mesozoic
d. Neoproterozoic

4. Extinction (Extinct)
When an animal species has died out and no longer exists, except as fossils
(PAGES 7, 10, 14, 40–41, 49, 56)

Which animals are NOT extinct?
a. Dodo bird
b. Monarch butterfly
c. Passenger pigeon
d. Komodo dragon

5. Fossils
The remains of plants and animals from millions of years ago
(PAGES 7, 10, 14, 16–17, 22, 27, 29, 30–31, 36–37, 48, 50–51, 56)

Which is NOT commonly found as a fossil?
a. Wood
b. Bone
c. Eyeballs
d. Teeth

6. Habitat
The place and natural condition in which an animal lives
(PAGES 12–13, 18–19, 29, 30–31)

Which is NOT a habitat?
a. Forest
b. Your room
c. Swamp
d. Cave

7. Herbivore
An animal with a diet consisting mostly of plants
(PAGES 28–29, 56)

Which dinosaurs were herbivores?
a. *Brachiosaurus*
b. *Stegosaurus*
c. *Allosaurus*
d. *Nothronychus*

8. Ornithischia
A large group of mostly plant-eating dinosaurs known for having bird-like hips, meaning they had hip bones that pointed down and back
(PAGES 11, 34)

Which three dinosaurs are ornithischia dinosaurs?
a. *Pachycephalosaurus*
b. *Tarchia*
c. *Diplodocus*
d. *Ankylosaurus*

9. Predator
An animal that hunts other animals for food
(PAGES 12–13, 18–19, 25, 28, 38–39, 49)

Which dinosaur was a predator?
a. *Seismosaurus*
b. *Argentinosaurus*
c. *Velociraptor*
d. *Leaellynasaura*

10. Reptiles
Cold-blooded vertebrates, meaning they have a backbone, that typically lay eggs and have scales
(PAGES 10, 22, 41, 52–53, 56)

Which animal is a reptile?
a. Salamander
b. Shark
c. Turtle
d. Armadillo

11. Saurischia
A large group of dinosaurs with lizard-like hips, meaning they had hip bones that pointed forward, that included all meat eaters and large plant eaters
(PAGES 11, 35)

Which two dinosaurs are saurischia dinosaurs?
a. *Triceratops*
b. *Ankylosaurus*
c. *Spinosaurus*
d. *Herrerasaurus*

12. Sauropods
Large, plant-eating dinosaurs that walked on four legs and are known for having long necks and tails
(PAGES 13, 22, 28, 38, 42)

Which dinosaur is a sauropod?
a. *Muttaburrasaurus*
b. *Brachiosaurus*
c. *Velociraptor*
d. *Struthiomimus*

13. Thyreophorans
Armored dinosaurs that typically walked on four legs and, along with their armor, had clubbed or spiked tails for defense against predators
(PAGES 28, 34, 38)

Which dinosaurs were thyreophorans?
a. *Microraptor*
b. *Stegosaurus*
c. *Minmi*
d. *Troodon*

14. Theropods
Meat-eating dinosaurs that walked on two legs
(PAGES 17, 26–27, 35, 38–39, 53)

Which dinosaur is a theropod?
a. *Iguanodon*
b. *Ankylosaurus*
c. *Spinosaurus*
d. *Diplodocus*

ANSWERS:
1. a and c (Iguanodon could walk on four and two legs); 2. a and c; 3. c; 4. b and d; 5. c; 6. b; 7. a, b, and d; 8. a, b, and d; 9. c; 10. c; 11. c and d; 12. b; 13. b and c; 14. c.

FIND OUT MORE

Want to dig deeper on prehistoric life? Try these resources to learn more about dinosaurs.

DINO DOCUMENTARIES

The Great Dinosaur Escape (2011)
by National Geographic

History Classics: Dinosaurs! (2008)
by the History Channel

When Dinosaurs Ruled the Earth (2011)
by the Discovery Channel

"DINO-RIFFIC" READS

National Geographic Kids Ultimate Dinopedia: The Most Complete Dinosaur Reference Ever
By Don Lessum
National Geographic Children's Books, 2010.

National Geographic Dinosaurs
By Paul Barrett
National Geographic Children's Books, 2001.

WEBSITES

Kids: Ask your parents for permission to search online.

www.bbc.co.uk/sn/prehistoric_life/dinosaurs
Browse through fantastic images and read about prehistoric life.

www.nps.gov/dino/forkids/index.htm
You can learn about national parks and download a copy of the Junior Ranger Activity Book.

www.pbskids.org/games/dinosaurs.html
Check out the site's dinosaur games and field guide, from PBS Kids.

PLACES TO VISIT

American Museum of Natural History, New York, New York, U.S.A.

Dinosaur National Monument, Dinosaur, Colorado, U.S.A.

Dinosaur State Park, Rocky Hill, Connecticut, U.S.A.

Iziko Museum, Cape Town, South Africa

National Dinosaur Museum, Nicholls, Australian Capital Territory, Australia

Natural History Museum, London, United Kingdom

Natural History Museum of Los Angeles County, Los Angeles, California, U.S.A.

Naturkunde Museum, Berlin, Germany

Royal Tyrrell Museum, Drumheller, Alberta, Canada

Smithsonian Museum of Natural History, Washington, D.C., U.S.A.

BOLDFACE INDICATES ILLUSTRATIONS.

Acknowledgments: Special thanks to Rodolfo Coria, Ph.D., Institute of Paleobiology and Geology, National University of Río Negro, Argentina

Published by the National Geographic Society
John M. Fahey, *Chairman of the Board and Chief Executive Officer*
Declan Moore, *Executive Vice President; President, Publishing and Travel*
Melina Gerosa Bellows, *Executive Vice President; Chief Creative Officer, Books, Kids, and Family*

Prepared by the Book Division
Hector Sierra, *Senior Vice President and General Manager*
Nancy Laties Feresten, *Senior Vice President, Kids Publishing and Media*
Jennifer Emmett, *Vice President, Editorial Director, Children's Books*
Eva Absher-Schantz, *Design Director, Kids Publishing and Media*
Jay Sumner, *Director of Photography, Children's Publishing*
R. Gary Colbert, *Production Director*
Jennifer A. Thornton, *Director of Managing Editorial*

NG Staff for This Book
Robin Terry, *Project Editor*
James Hiscott, Jr., *Art Director*
Lori Epstein, *Senior Photo Editor*
Ariane Szu-Tu, *Editorial Assistant*
Callie Broaddus, *Design Production Assistant*
Margaret Leist, *Photo Assistant*
Carl Mehler, *Director of Maps*
Grace Hill, *Associate Managing Editor*
Michael O'Connor, *Production Editor*
Lewis R. Bassford, *Production Manager*
Susan Borke, *Legal and Business Affairs*

Production Services
Phillip L. Schlosser, *Senior Vice President*
Chris Brown, *Vice President, NG Book Manufacturing*
George Bounelis, *Senior Production Manager*
Nicole Elliot, *Director of Production*
Rachel Faulise, *Manager*
Robert L. Barr, *Manager*

Editorial, Design, and Production by Plan B Book Packagers

Captions
Cover: A *Yangchuanosaurus* runs after its prey.
Back cover: (rt) *Albertosaurus* was a scrappy theropod dinosaur. (le) *Corythosaurus*, or "helmet lizard," was a duck-billed dinosaur.
Page 1: A *Sarcosuchus*, or SuperCroc makes a surprise attack on a dinosaur.
Page 2: The skull of this Antarctic beauty, *Cryolophosaurus*, was discovered 100 miles (161 km) from the South Pole. It had a bony crest on its head.

The National Geographic Society is one of the world's largest nonprofit scientific and educational organizations. Founded in 1888 to "increase and diffuse geographic knowledge," the Society's mission is to inspire people to care about the planet. It reaches more than 400 million people worldwide each month through its official journal, National Geographic, and other magazines; National Geographic Channel; television documentaries; music; radio; films; books; DVDs; maps; exhibitions; live events; school publishing programs; interactive media; and merchandise. National Geographic has funded more than 10,000 scientific research, conservation and exploration projects and supports an education program promoting geographic literacy.

For more information, please visit nationalgeographic.com, call 1-800-NGS LINE (647-5463), or write to the following address:
National Geographic Society
1145 17th Street N.W.
Washington, D.C. 20036-4688 U.S.A.

Visit us online at nationalgeographic.com/books

For librarians and teachers: ngchildrensbooks.org

More for kids from National Geographic:
kids.nationalgeographic.com

For information about special discounts for bulk purchases, please contact National Geographic Books Special Sales: ngspecsales@ngs.org

For rights or permissions inquiries, please contact National Geographic Books Subsidiary Rights: ngbookrights@ngs.org

Paperback ISBN: 978-1-4263-1496-4
Reinfored library binding ISBN: 978-1-4263-1497-1

Printed in Hong Kong
14/THK/1